TEACH ME HOW TO PROSPER

by Tariq Price

World Overcomers Church Int'l
Senior Pastor & Founder
&
Born To Win Ministries
President

www.iwasborntowin.org

Teach Me How To Prosper

Copyright © 2012 by Tariq Price

ISBN 978-0-616-73093-6

Dedication

I want to dedicate this book to my wife ShaRease Price she has truly been encouraging and inspirational in my life, and because she believes in me I have the courage and belief I can conquer anything. I especially want to thank my spiritual parents Dr. Rick V. Layton and Dr. Barbara Layton. I appreciate them for pouring into my life continuously. Dr. Layton has demonstrated what it truly means to be a Godly husband and father, a Pastor, a spiritual father, a mentor, and a man of integrity who walks upright. If it wasn't for the connection, impartation and their covering, I wouldn't be where I am today.

Unless otherwise indicated Scripture quotations are taken from the King James Version Bible.

Scripture quotations marked AMP are taken from the Amplified Bible

Scripture quotations marked NLT are taken from the New Living Translation Bible

Scripture quotations marked MSG are taken from the Message Bible

Contents

Introduction

It was early in my walk with the Lord when I discovered some missing pieces of my family's total prosperity. I was at a point where I couldn't seem to make things happen in our lives in regards to prospering. I began to search out for answers. I eventually got a hold of teachings on prosperity, which a majority came from listening to a whole lot of Dr. Rick V. Layton who is my spiritual father, Dr. Leroy Thompson Sr., Bro. Kenneth Copeland, Kenneth E. Hagin, and Dr. Creflo A. Dollar, who is my spiritual grandfather. These men are the ones I primarily glean to for answers and who I know in my heart that are prospering and walking it out and living in it based on their fruit. There are definitely more individuals whom I watched on television broadcasts and read books from but these men listed are those who have really helped to get me started on my journey of success in every area. My wife ShaRease and I are walking in total prosperity to a degree that it seems unreal. We have an anointing for healing, business, finances, and to help cause hundreds and thousands to increase in any area they need increase in. So in this book I pray that you get answers on how to prosper in every area of your life. I have been called by God to teach Total Healing to the Body of Christ. I pray that you will enjoy this book, and please allow the Holy Spirit to teach *you* how to prosper!

Where Does Prosperity Originate From?

Ask yourself, "where does prosperity originate from?" Prosperity originates from God. All of who God is encompasses prosperity. Everything God does always prospers. You and I come from the mouth or DNA of God. Once you and I became born again you and I were born into prosperity. It may not seem like it in the natural, but that's why He gave us the measure of faith to access it according to Romans 12:3:

For I say, through the grace given unto me, to every man that is among you, not to think of himself more highly than he ought to think; but to think soberly, according as God hath dealt to every man the measure of faith.

He gave you and I *the* measure of faith. You may be asking, "what is faith Pastor Price?" Faith is your confidence and your belief in the Word of God. Faith is simply acting on the Word of God. I like to tell my congregation that God is not impressed by what you intend to do, He is impressed by what you actually do. It is in your doing that God is pleased. Doing what Pastor Price? You do by literally doing His Word, in speaking His word, in confessing His Word which is declaring the same thing that the Word of God says. Your doing is also in believing His Word, standing firmly on His Word, sleeping with and waking up to His Word. It's simple, you and I cannot separate from His Word. Joshua 1:8 says:

This book of the law shall not depart out of thy mouth; but thou shalt meditate therein day and night, that thou mayest observe to do according to all that is written therein: for then thou shalt make thy way prosperous, and then thou shalt have good success.

So this scripture says that if we *do not* separate from the Word, then we shall MAKE our way prosperous, and THEN we shall have good success, not bad success but good success!

My job in this book is to show you that you are a success and you were born to succeed in life. You were born to win in every area of your life. Satan's job is to keep you in religion, which is bondage, his job is to keep you thinking that you can't move up in this life, his job is to keep you in fear which is satan's force and contaminates your faith. Fear stagnates your faith, it keeps it from moving. The world that we live in minimizes or limits prosperity just to money, and that's just one piece of the prosperity pie. In this book we're going to talk about kingdom prosperity and where it originates from. Amen? I need everybody reading this to be soaring. I need everybody reading this to be winning in life. Say this with me, "I Am A Winner!"

Reader, the Spirit of the Lord told me that this is your season that you are getting ready to break through, and you're going to break through strongly. The Lord advised me to release to you that you're going to break through so much it's going to be mind-blowing. I hear the Spirit also saying, that it's your time to rise up and shine! According to Isaiah 60 in the name of Jesus, you go ahead and break through. Glory to God!

You Prosper By the Renewing Of The Mind

You cannot move towards prosperity without the seed of God's word. Are you aware that the Bible is a book full of seed? The incorruptible Word which is seed has the ability to grow any harvest you need in your life if you decide to plant the Word in your heart. You cannot move towards prosperity without the seed of God's Word first entering your life. You have to get the seed of God's Word first and let it enter into your life. The Word provides the light that is needed to break the chains of poverty. The Word provides the light that is needed to break the chains of stress, chains of cancer, chains of anything satan tries to bring you. The Word will break it, The Word will slice it up with its power. Hebrews 4:12 says:

For the word of God is quick, and powerful, and sharper than any two-edged sword, piercing even to the dividing asunder of soul and spirit, and of the joints and marrow, and is a discerner of the thoughts and intents of the heart.

The Word can destroy all power and schemes the enemy tries to throw at you. With prosperity your first concern must be the prosperity of your soul. You may be asking, what is your soul? Your soul is your mind, will and emotions. Your first concern must be the prosperity of your mind which determines your position in life. When your mind or your soul is prospering that means your mind is being fed good seed from the Word of God which produces good harvest. Yes, the Word of God is the best seed or food you can feed your mind. When your mind is prospering, you will see results that are tangible. You will then begin to see results manifest quickly and powerfully. The Word of God has the ability to uproot bad thinking and replace those bad thoughts with the Word of God. This will only happen if and when you decide to renew or renovate your thoughts and start thinking on prosperity or in other words, The Word. Prosperity is not just money, and money will never be total prosperity according to the Kingdom. In the kingdom of God, prosperity is defined as being rich or abundantly supplied in every area of your life. In the Kingdom of God, prosperity means total completeness in every area of your life.

It's disappointing that the world defines prosperity as just money and that will never be true for the believer. Some churches, Pastors and spiritual leaders have also lacked in defining total prosperity with defining prosperity as just money. Have you seen or heard this before? Total prosperity is being whole, wealthy in every area. The whole pie. Nothing missing. Nothing broken, and plenty more to be put in store. Are you getting this?

God's Word is your foundation. His Word is the foundation for prosperity. Not only is the Word your seed for harvesting prosperity, it's also the water that nourishes your financial, healing, and well-being seeds in order for them to grow. When you speak the Word of God you are watering or reinforcing what you believe. You must understand that the sowing of your time, your offerings, your returning of your tithes to God still needs The Word of God to water what you have believed God to manifest. So when you're tithing and you're sowing seed, allow the Word to water that which you are believing God for by opening up your mouth and speaking the uncompromised Word of God. Please know that you can sow all you have, and you can tithe on all your increase but you cannot sow or give without having the ultimate seed along with it which is the Word. Without the Word, no seed can grow. Am I helping you? This is for everybody who believes. Mark 9:23 says:

Jesus said unto him, If thou canst believe, all things are possible to him that believeth.

So let's recap, your financial seeds need water, which is the Word, in order for it to grow. Are you getting this? Are you really standing on this all week long? Romans 13:8 says:

Owe no man anything, but to love one another: for he that loveth another hath fulfilled the law.

I consistently speak over our lives and thank God that my wife and I are totally debt free and the only debt we have is the debt of love. God desires for you and I to live this way. Not to be concerned about anything. You have been given the power: His ability on your ability that causes you to prosper and get wealth. So your power is necessary, it is the necessary element to move you from one place in your life to another. Power is necessary. The anointing is necessary, it is the necessary element to move you from where you are to your next place. It's time to get your stuff! It's time to live like you were intended to live.

It's the power or the anointing that's going to cause you to move into your next house, to your next career, and to your next level of success. Well, where is the next place or level? First, you must understand that in the spirit you are already at the top. You've got to decide to see yourself already at the top. Ephesians 2: 6 says:

And hath raised us up together, and made us sit together in heavenly places in Christ Jesus.

See you are already there in the spirit, so now work the plan out God has given you for your life so that it may manifest in the natural, in your own lane and on your own level. People at the top, who think they have "arrived" in the natural sometimes get unreachable, then they become unteachable. They then think they have reached a certain plateau so nobody can tell them anything anymore. Say this, "I'm going to keep enjoying where I am." So you enjoy where you are and let God take you to your next place while you're at the top with Him. Simply enjoy your journey. Stop stressing out trying to get to the destination. You're already there. You have to see yourself already at that place called there. You must keep moving while you're enjoying where you are. Why? Because you are a kingdom citizen. Ephesians 2:6 just stated you're already seated at the right hand of the Father. You are already there. So just allow Him to increase you, knowing that you are already at the top. Always know, first you must see yourself at the top in the spirit before you'll ever see yourself on the top in the natural. When you know you are at the top in the spirit with Him you won't lose your soul trying to get somewhere in the natural, you'll simply yield to the power and work God's plan for your life.

Deuteronomy 8:17-18 says:

[17]And thou say in thine heart, My power and the might of mine hand hath gotten me this

*wealth.*¹⁸ *But thou shalt remember the* LORD *thy God: for it is he that giveth thee power to get wealth, that he may establish his covenant which he sware unto thy fathers, as it is this day.*

Who shall we remember? The Lord thy God is who we remember who has given us the power to get wealth, or move to another level. Power is translated to the anointing. The anointing is what causes you to increase. What is the anointing? It's the burden removing, yoke destroying power of God. The anointing will remove poverty. It'll remove anything that is of satan that's attacking and disrupting your life. The anointing will also attract the things of God to you.

So God has given you power or the anointing to get wealth, so you must arise or change your posture and position in order for prosperity to manifest itself in your life. Isaiah 60:1 says:

Arise, shine; for thy light is come, and the glory of the LORD *is risen upon thee.*

This is our time to shine. It's time! It's time for us to rise up and take back what the enemy has stolen from us. The scripture says, "Arise, shine for thy light is come and the glory! Oh my goodness! Please know that the mentioning of glory in this scripture isn't that halo that you see in cartoons. The Word is speaking of manifestation! I previously declared to you , that it's your time to shine. That means its manifestation time for the believer. Understand that without the light, the light of God's Word, you will stay the same. With no Word, you stay the same. If you are born again, you are the seed of Abraham and have a right to the promises of God and to see them unfold and manifest in your life. Galatians 3:29 says:

And if ye be Christ's, then are ye Abraham's seed, and heirs according to the promise.

You are the seed of Abraham and you have the right to all the promises. You have a right to all the healings, to all the wealth, to all the promotion, to all the increase, and to all the favor of God. You have a right to all of that. Why? It was promised to you. He promised you healing, He promised you victory, He promised you abundance, He promised you victory all the time by the renewing of your mind, He promised you a healthy marriage. He also promised that He would increase you more and more you and your children according to Psalms 115:14. You have a God given right to be successful. And listen; don't apologize for your success. Don't apologize for the financial increase you're about to experience from God. God's blessing you, don't apologize for it. Tell the whole world what the Lord is doing for you. That's exactly how you position yourself to be a vessel of God to win the world. That's how you win your sick, broke, busted and disgusted friends and family too. The Body of Christ should be declaring things such as: "I was diagnosed with cancer, and now I'm free of it!"; "I had symptoms of sugar diabetes and now my blood is normal!" Are you getting this? Be ready to declare the goodness of God in your life. When you continue to give God glory, He's going to continue to give you glory in the Earth. Think about that. You just need to get into God, and you then give Him access to fill you up. He is going to continually add to your life and never stop increasing you. You are going to stay in the flow of God, which will cause you to overflow. When you decide to fill yourself up with the Word, what do you think He's going do to you? He's going to fill you up with His goodness. If you are lazy and don't want to get in your bible and discover who you are and the promises that belong to you, you can't partake of God's goodness to its maximum capacity. People who are lazy and they want to complain about what they don't have and consistently fuss about what they are lacking will always find themselves lacking. All they have to do is dive into the Word of God, and began thinking and speaking the Word of God and things have to change on their behalf. The Word changes things. Whatever you need will just show itself up somewhere, some way and somehow. All you have to do is believe.

I constantly dream and meditate about speaking all across the world and again and again it' happening. You may be thinking, how are they finding out about you? I honestly don't know, and I really don't care, it's a part of my dream and God is able to bring it to pass. I know His purpose for my life. I was called to spread the gospel to the uttermost parts of the Earth. And if you are a tither and pushing forth your local ministry and other ministries, you are spreading the gospel too. You don't need a pulpit to spread the gospel. All you need is God's plan for your life.

God will set you up to where you don't have to pay for anything. His favor will take care of everything. It's certainly happening in the Body of Christ. When you embrace true prosperity you are truly blessed to be a blessing. People of the body of Christ are giving away cars, airplanes, paying off churches for pastors, and so much more. This is definitely what the whole body of Christ should be doing so it can become easier to spread the gospel. We must rise up and be the givers who we were predestined to be. We should desire to give because we love people unconditionally, with no strings attached. This is the goodness of God. This is how the body of Christ is supposed to be.

You don't have to know as much Word as me, or your pastor or your friends, just know what you know and He'll increase you on your level. Are you getting this? Say, "It's my time to shine!" Glory to God! It is indeed your time to shine. The Body has been without in the Earth long enough. We have to acknowledge He is manifesting Himself in and on our lives daily.

Listen, you don't have to look for things in order to receive. He might give you an idea. I was flying one day and thought about the fact that I was flying in somebody else's idea. All it takes is one idea from God. An idea has the potential to transform and change your life and others lives! I began to pray that the Lord would give me an idea that will impact generations. I began to cry out to Him, "Speak to me!" You see we have to start thinking about the manifestations that are in our ideas! Think about it, you eat your food off an utensil which was somebody's idea. The food you eat is derived from somebody's idea to raise some cattle and plant some crops. You see how we must stop missing it in the Body of Christ? If you're a tither, God promises that He WILL open up the windows of heaven and pour you out a blessing. What He's talking about is here is an anointing for witty inventions, ideas and concepts. Always know that once God gives you an idea, it's already blessed. Once you get the idea, all you have to do is move towards it, and be confident that He'll send the people, buildings, finances and support you need.

So let's recap, if you are born again, you are the seed of Abraham and have a right to the promises of God. You have the right to be a millionaire.   I believe that every person reading this book will experience the goodness of God this year if you will only believe.

Know Your Lane

It's vitally important to know your lane in your own life. You must allow the Holy Spirit to minister to you what season you are always in. Your lane is the roadmap God has strategically laid out for your success in life. You must be aware that no one has the same lane in life as you. When you recognize your lane and stay in it, you will be successful wherever you are, and you will be the best in whatever you do. It doesn't matter if you are working at a cheeseburger factory. Because you are in your lane you are empowered to be the best cheeseburger worker there is. Often times, people discredit the lane they're in and try to drive in someone else's which will eventually lead to destruction. When you decide to embrace your lane in this life, you'll quickly begin to enjoy yourself. See, in your lane, the right relationships have to show up. It is necessary for you to realize and know you have to leave certain people in certain seasons so the right ones can come in your new season. You must get from around some people; because everybody can't go to the destination in this life you've been promised. Some may ask, "why must people keep hating on me?" Some do because they simply can't go where you are going. It's important to know many people already see the success on your life and often times when people see success on you at such an awesome level, they don't really see it on themselves. Unfortunately, when some recognize the success on you they want to talk about you and turn their noses up at you. It's sad that they don't know all they have to do is begin to get into the Word of God like you and begin to find out their purpose in this life and who they really are in Christ Jesus. I charge you to keep walking with your shoulders up, and know that God is going to take care of you. Walk with your head held high. Psalms 35:27 says:

Let them shout for joy, and be glad, that favour my righteous cause: yea, let them say continually,

*Let the LORD be magnified, which hath pleasure
in the prosperity of his servant.*

Aren't you his servant? He says that He takes
pleasure in *your* prosperity, because He is
magnified in it. When you magnify God and tell
about his goodness He takes pleasure in that. I
believe all parent(s) or guardian(s) loves when
their children exalt them for what they have
blessed them with. Likewise, it's the same with
our Heavenly Father. When you get a raise and
you go tell somebody and give them hope that
they can receive one too, God gets magnified.
And then you know what He does when He get
magnified? He zero's in on you again with the
magnifying glass, and loads you up with some
more goodness. Don't shut up about the goodness
of God. Go tell it. Go tell it. Let the Lord be
magnified in it. Why? Because God takes
pleasure in it. God is interested in total life
prosperity, which includes, but is not limited to
just money. Total life prosperity is *shalom,* which
means peace. So from hereon reprogram your

mind to think peace when you hear the word prosperity. Shalom means continual well- being as success. So prosperity can't be bad if God takes pleasure in it. I believe the people who preach against prosperity are more than likely broke and in many areas of their lives they have no peace. I believe that when you're married and you come home and can't get a kiss on the cheek, you're broke in the area of relationships which is a part of total prosperity. Some times I ask the question of why married people struggle so much. I believe it's because of pride. Both parties just need to make a decision to just get it right and forgive! Many married couples continue to hold on to grudges and foolishly sleep on one side of the bed alone, which is just lonely. And they can't even sleep because they're pondering on the issues. Total prosperity has the gift of forgiveness for oneself and others.

One may have millions and millions of dollars in the bank and yet lack healing in your body. Well, in this case you're just a man or woman with lots of money but sick physically, which means you're not truly rich. To be truly rich is to have nothing missing, and nothing broken and plenty in every area of your life.

When your friend is sick, in the name of Jesus you have the power to lay hands, because you are walking around with the blessing and you're walking around knowing your authority in Jesus' Name. Please know that Jesus restored all of the pieces of the prosperity pie. Let's picture prosperity as a pie. If you are missing a piece in your life, find out what that piece is so it can be restored by the Restorer, Jesus. When Jesus came, He came to seek and save the loss. Jesus came to give us life in abundance. John 10:10 says:

The thief cometh not, but for to steal, and to kill, and to destroy: I am come that they might have life, and that they might have it more abundantly.

So the believer's whole pie has been restored, and we have to see it like that. Nothing should be missing out of our pie, not even one piece. Once we start seeing it like that, it's going to be like that in the natural. Jesus came in the Earth to preach the gospel to the poor. Matthew 11:4-5 says:

Jesus answered and said to them, "Go and tell John the things which you hear and see: The blind see and the lame walk; the lepers are cleansed and the deaf hear; the dead are raised up and the poor have the gospel preached to them.

Poor means to lack something that's needed. My definition of poor is *Passing Over Opportunities Repeatedly.* It says Jesus answered and said unto them go and show John again those things which you do here and see. This scripture further confirms that it is possible to be rich in material assets and poor in other areas in your life. Let's go to Revelations 3:17. It says:

Because thou sayest, I am rich, and increased with goods, and have need of nothing; and knowest not that thou art wretched, and miserable, and poor, and blind, and naked:

So let's recap: Although a person may be financially wealthy, he or she may be lacking meaningful relationships, or, dying of cancer or possibly have no peace of mind. Clearly, the whole pie isn't there.

We as spirit beings, born-again believers have to be rich in the mind. 3 John 2 says:

I wish above all things that thou mayest prosper, that thou mayest prosper, that thou mayest prosper and be in health, even as thy soul prospers.

So you see that? The prosperity of your soul which consists of your mind, will and emotions must be your first priority. Soul prosperity comes from revelation of God's word. Your prosperity comes from the revelation you receive from God's word. So if you are down on your luck, it is not because of luck, you are lacking the light of God's

Word. As believers we are not to even believe in luck. You must realize you're lacking because you are lacking the light of God's word. If you are down in any area in your life, it's because you are lacking the Word on the issue.

When you have God's word on the issue, you have God on the issue. It is impossible, for you not to prosper when the Word is in operation in your life. When the Word is moving in your life, it's impossible for you to fail. When you are consistently getting and acting on the Word it's impossible for you to not prosper. I know and believe that you can be as healthy as you desire to be, with applying and working out the Word and with working out at the gym. I believe every marriage can be as successful as it's desired to be. I believe you can be rich with good friends that will encourage you and tell you that can do it and are assets to you going to your next level. Being rich in relationships is key to moving ahead, simply because God uses people to accomplish His will in the earth. Whenever God is getting ready to bless you He does it through a person. Whenever heaven decides to promote you, God always does it through an individual. That's why it's always important to treat people right all the time. Never allow yesterday people who are those that try to come in your life and put you back in your past life. Remember you are a new creature according to 2 Corinthians 5:17 because you are in Christ, so embrace your new relationships for your future. The Apostle Paul said in 2 Corinthians 7:1-4:

Having therefore these promises, dearly beloved, let us cleanse ourselves from all filthiness of the flesh and spirit, perfecting holiness in the fear of God. Receive us; we have wronged no man, we have corrupted no man, we have defrauded no man. I speak not this to condemn you: for I have said before, that ye are in our hearts to die and live with you. Great is my boldness of speech toward you, great is my glorying of you: I am filled with comfort, I am exceeding joyful in all our tribulation.

Paul clearly declared he had wronged no man. Know that you are a new creature headed into all that God has for you, and it's your time to prosper God's way.

The Power of God's Word's

There is nothing, absolutely nothing in Earth and in your life that can't be turned around by your words. It doesn't matter how powerful something may seem in your life, you can turn any situation into a different direction with the words you speak. Think about it, the worlds were framed by God speaking it to existence. Hebrews 11: 3 says:

Through faith we understand that the worlds were framed by the word of God, so that things which are seen were not made of things which do appear.

The scripture is showing us that the world we live in was created by the words of God! That's something to get excited about. Why? Because the same ability that God used to create the world is the same ability He deposited into us when we became born-again. So, we have the power already, to open up our mouths and speak the Word of God and see positive results happen.

Glory to God! The entire course of nature (past present, and future) and the circumstances surrounding every person are being controlled by that person's words. I've come to understand, you and I don't have a choice whether or not we live by words, God has already predestined for us to do so, but we do have a choice of what words we decide to choose. We must continually make the decision to speak the Word of God which is the truth for our lives and see things move in our favor, opposed to speaking the negative words of satan which are lies and see our lives broken and hurting in areas.

If your mouth will feed your heart the Word of God when you don't need it, then your heart will feed your mouth the Word of God when you do need it. Make sense? Here's what that means. There will be times where everything seems to be alright in every area of your life, but that's not the time to relax on the Word, you must still continuously feed your heart or your spirit the Word. So when you are in a situation the Word of

God that has been deposited in your heart will be there to rescue you out of that problem. What you decide to meditate on long enough will eventually come out of your mouth. And what comes out of your mouth will frame your life.

Every time you open your mouth and release the Word of God out of your mouth you are appropriating what is yours in Christ. We are to confess what we can do in Christ, who we are in Christ, and what we have in Christ. Remember through Jesus, it's a finished work.

We have to speak God's Word! Let's make a decision not to speak what we want to say but to speak what the Word says. Isaiah 58:13 says:

If thou turn away thy foot from the sabbath, from doing thy pleasure on my holy day; and call the sabbath a delight, the holy of the LORD, honourable; and shalt honour him, not doing thine own ways, nor finding thine own pleasure, nor speaking thine own words:

You see, many times we desire to speak and do what we want to do, but the scripture is telling us to honor God in what we say by deciding to speak His word only. His Word is what will cut through whatever you're going through.

Hebrews 4:12 (AMP) says:

For the Word that God speaks is alive and full of power [making it active, operative, energizing, and effective]; it is sharper than any two-edged sword, penetrating to the dividing line of the [a]breath of life (soul) and [the immortal] spirit, and of joints and marrow [of the deepest parts of our nature], exposing and sifting and analyzing and judging the very thoughts and purposes of the heart.

Now, let's read Psalm 17:4 (AMP) it says:

Concerning the works of men, by the word of Your lips I have avoided the ways of the violent (the paths of the destroyer).

This scripture is confirming the importance of recognizing that our words are vital and they will make our lives or break them. Proverbs 18:20-21 says:

A man's belly shall be satisfied with the fruit of his mouth; and with the increase of his lips shall he be filled. Death and life are in the power of the tongue: and they that love it shall eat the fruit thereof.

Whatever we decide to release out of our mouths will develop fruit, either good fruit or bad fruit. Our words are the way God's will, purpose, and desires are released to become a reality. Faith- filled words will put you over and above in this life. Fear-filled words will put you under and beneath. Your words are spiritual containers that carry power. They can carry love and faith or words can carry hate and fear. Remember, God gave us the ability or power to create just like Him. Genesis 1:26 says:

And God said, Let us make man in our image, after our likeness: and let them have dominion over the fish of the sea, and over the fowl of the air, and over the cattle, and over all the earth,

41

and over every creeping thing that creepeth upon the earth.

Words are the process starters in your life. What kind of processes do you need? A healing process? A new relationship process? A stronger financial process? Only your words can start the total prosperity that you desire, you have to simply call it in.

Romans 4:17 says:

(As it is written, I have made thee a father of many nations,) before him whom he believed, even God, who quickeneth the dead, and calleth those things which be not as though they were.

We have to constantly call those things which be not as though they were in the natural. How do you call something? That's right, with words. Your words are the building blocks that construct or build your life, both present and future. Before you start the process of building make sure you have the Word to build yout new life with. You may not be pleased with the outcome of some areas of your life, but don't get discouraged. Your words can build up whatever you've allowed words to tear down in the past. Your words can restore. Your words can restructure whatever in your life that may need a renovation. Words have creative ability; they create everything you see in the natural realm. Remember, things which are seen were made up of things not seen. You surely can't see words as they come out of your mouth but eventually you will see the fruit of what you've said in the natural. Go ahead and speak God's Word. God's Word is the incorruptible seed, which has in it the ability and DNA to cause itself to come to pass. This means that the Word of God has in it the makeup to create the house or the car you need. Or maybe you need a better attitude, stronger marriage, or a new career. The decision is on you, just decide to speak the Word of God and watch your life transform!

Agreeing With God

What does it mean to agree with God? To agree with God is to simply believe and know that His Word is true. To agree with God is to decide to be on His team, which is the winning team. Abraham chose to believe God, regardless of any circumstances that were going on in the natural. He chose not to focus on what he was feeling. He made a conscious decision to believe the report of the Lord about His future. He didn't listen to what his relatives said neither his coworkers, he believed the Most High God. Let's take a look at Romans 4:18-21. It says:

Who against hope believed in hope, that he might become the father of many nations, according to that which was spoken, So shall thy seed be. And being not weak in faith, he considered not his own body now dead, when he was about an hundred years old, neither yet the deadness of Sarah's womb: He staggered not at the promise of God through unbelief; but was strong in faith, giving glory to God; And being

44

fully persuaded that, what he had promised, he was able also to perform.

According to, in the Greek means a Hearty Agreement. It also means total, complete, unquestioning, unreserved agreement. To totally agree means to have no ifs, ands, or buts about it. Verse 20 says He staggered not at the promise of God through unbelief. Abraham did not believe the report of the doctors, he did not look at his age, Abraham agreed with God and that was it. All you need to do is believe God and get on board with His plan for your life. It's important that you never try to get God on board with your plans. Look at verse 21 it says "he was so fully persuaded that what God had promised in His Word, He was totally able to perform". Sons and Daughters of God, He is well able to heal you from any sickness and disease. God is well able to get you out of debt. All you need is a plan of action from God and that plan will show you how to get out of whatever you're in. God is well able to favor you before Him and before men. God is well able to shrink cysts, cure anyone from AIDS or HIV and so much more, whatever you're willing to be in agreement with in the Word. Abraham was in hearty agreement with what God had spoken to him about being the father of many nations. He knew it and no one else had to tell him that. God told him, and Abraham had total peace about the situation. Abraham was fully persuaded we have to be just like Abraham. We have to take God at His Word and know that when God speaks something to you He is well able to accomplish it through you.

For example, if God told you to build a building, you should be totally convinced that He's going to do it. He's going to make sure you have the right architects, the right materials you need, the right contractors, and the right finances! Glory to God! Your agreement with His plan releases the manifestations to begin in this Earth on your behalf. Romans 4:18 (MSG) says:

When everything was hopeless, Abraham believed anyway, deciding to live not on the basis of what he saw he couldn't do but on what God said he would do. And so he was made father of a multitude of peoples. God himself said to him, "You're going to have a big family, Abraham!"

You've got to believe that you're going to have an abundant life, because God said you're going to have an abundant life. I speak everyday that I am in total agreement with what God has told me and called me to do. I encourage you to do the same. Deuteronomy 8:17-18 (MSG) says:

If you start thinking to yourselves, "I did all this. And all by myself. I'm rich. It's all mine!"— well, think again. Remember that GOD, your God, gave you the strength to produce all this wealth so as to confirm the covenant that he promised to your ancestors—as it is today.

The Word tells us to *remember*. Another word for remember is to recall. It's important to recall where you were once at in life and know that because the power of God invaded your life you are now at a different place. We must remember the One who spoke the dreams to us. We must remember the One who have gave us the ability or power at the beginning that caused and is causing us to increase more and more. Always know that God gives you the power to get wealth to further His Kingdom which is the Kingdom of God. Deuteronomy 28: 2 says:

And all these blessings shall come on thee, and overtake thee, if thou shalt hearken unto the voice of the LORD thy God.

Did you see that? *All* these blessings shall come on you and me and overtake us if we just hearken to the voice of God. His voice is His Word. Reader, this verse is talking about overflow. You are in the season in your life where God wants to set you up for more. He wants you to have excess. He wants you to be in abundance. He wants you to stay blessed so that all the blessings you need can come upon you. Another word for blessed is empowered. You stay empowered by staying connected to the power, which is the Word of God. When you stay in the Word you set yourself up to allow all the blessings of God to come upon you and to live a lifestyle of overflow. Are you ready to be overtaken by the goodness of God? Deuteronomy 28:8 says:

The LORD shall command the blessing upon thee in thy storehouses, and in all that thou settest thine hand unto; and he shall bless thee in the land which the LORD thy God giveth thee.

Lets zoom in the part where it says, "The Lord shall command the blessing upon thee in thy storehouses". Bless the Lord! He's talking about your bank accounts. Remember another word for blessing is empowerment. So God commands empowerment over your finances. Are you ready for increase, multiplication and strength in your finances? Let's read Deuteronomy 28:12. It says:

The LORD shall open unto thee his good treasure, the heaven to give the rain unto thy land in his season, and to bless all the work of thine hand: and thou shalt lend unto many nations, and thou shalt not borrow.

Verse 12 is saying The Lord has already opened up to us His good treasury. Thank God it's open for you and I. We just need to agree with God and open our mouths and call it in! Psalm 35:27 says:

Let them shout for joy, and be glad, that favour my righteous cause: yea, let them say continually, Let the LORD be magnified, which hath pleasure in the prosperity of his servant.

If God takes pleasure in you and I prospering, then it should not be a problem or issue to anyone else. If anyone else has a problem with the idea of you prospering tell that individual that no one can stop your prosperity. God has already called you prosperous, and once God says it, that settles it!

God takes pleasure in His children walking by faith and pleasing Him. He gets a kick out of us talking just like Him. When we have the same speech as God we will have results like God. Jeremiah 1:12 says:

Then said the LORD unto me, Thou hast well seen: for I will hasten my word to perform it.

God is watching over His Word to make sure is happens in this Earth. All we have to do is agree with what He said, let what He said become our language, and release His Word out of our mouths. God desires to make His Word happen in our lives. He's ready and willing to perform it.

According to Bing Dictionary the word perform means to accomplish something or to carry out an action. It also means to complete a task that's required. We should be confident in knowing that once we agree with the Word and speak it, it's a done deal because God must complete it. Let's take a look at Jeremiah 1:12 in the Amplified Bible. It says:

Then said the Lord to me, You have seen well, for I am alert and active, watching over My word to perform it.

This translation says He is ALERT and ACTIVE. God is actively seeking His Word to do it in your life. He is still on the move. He uses us to create things in the Earth. He uses us to call those things which be not as though they were. We are made in His image and we are suppose to agree Him through imitation of what He says and does. Let's read Psalm 36:8, it says:

They shall be abundantly satisfied with the fatness of thy house; and thou shalt make them drink of the river of thy pleasures.

Do you agree with the Word? or Do you often agree with what your situation is telling you. Yes, situations can talk to you. That's why we have to speak to the situations and tell them how big our God is instead of magnifying our situations and making them gods in our lives. Psalm 65:11 (NLT) says:

You crown the year with a bountiful harvest; even the hard pathways overflow with abundance.

The word bountiful in the Bing dictionary means generous: giving generously, abundant: in plentiful supply. Do you agree with this scripture pertaining to how your years are going to be? The scripture also says He will make even the hard pathways overflow with abundance. According to Bing Dictionary abundance means to have large amounts and plentiful quantities. Seems to me, that if we agree with what God says, than we will live like how God wants us to live. God wants us to have more than enough. Exceedingly more than what we need so we can be a blessing and distribution centers of His goodness.

Your Seed Will Change Your Financial Future

Lets' start at John 12:24(AMP) it says:

I assure you, most solemnly I tell you, Unless a grain of wheat falls into the earth and dies, it remains [just one grain; it never becomes more but lives] by itself alone. But if it dies, it produces many others and yields a rich harvest.

Your seed is designed to change your financial situation. Your seed has the ability to change all of the hardship you may be experiencing. Your seed has in it the capacity to produce according to its DNA or kind. For instance, if you take an apple and you open it up and recover an apple seed and plant the apple seed in the ground, it'll produce what? Oranges? Absolutely not! The apple seed can only produce more of its kind which is more apples. Your seed also needs good ground or rich soil to produce a harvest. Now, it's important to know that your seed is meant to be planted and when it produces a harvest, you then can enjoy or eat the harvest. If you were to eat an apple seed it is very bitter. It is better to eat the flesh or the fruit. Same as your financial seed, if you eat your seed it's bitter. Once eaten, it cannot produce what it's capable of producing. Why? Because you ate the seed. If you sow the seed and wait for the harvest and eat the fruit of the harvest which is more apples, it tastes good. I've realized that many people are eating their seed and it's causing them to have bitter results. If you learn how to sow your seed by faith and wait on the harvest, then you will have plenty to eat.

According to John 12:24(AMP) we previously read a seed must die, in order to produce more of its kind. Your seed must die to its purpose. And the purpose of your seed is to produce the harvest. When you're planting or sowing your seed make sure you're naming your seed. An awesome man of God, Dr. Leroy Thompson talks about money with a mission or seed with a mission. I've learned that your seed must have a purpose and must be moving. It's important for you to sow or give to individuals, institutions, or organizations that are also sowing seed. Your seed must be on the move. If you are a part of an institution that's not moving and not helping other people then it's possible that may not be the best soil to plant into. Good soil helps other people. Good soil helps other people produce. Good soil makes things easier for somebody. Are you getting this? Good soil will see someone who's without and make sure they are with. Sometimes you may not know what the best soil for your harvest is, but the Holy Ghost does. Ask Him to reveal to you the good soil you should be planting into.

Seed brings forth its purpose and destiny only when it's sown. If you hold on to your seed and never sow it you'll never experience the harvest of that seed. Seed contains within itself the supernatural design for increase. Often times people complain of having a lack of money. See when you spend money, there's no return of more money, because money alone cannot produce a harvest, but when you renew your mind and see money as seed, it can certainly produce more of its kind.

Maybe you've made foolish mistakes in the area of finances. It's okay, we all have, just simply repent and get it right. Ask God to minister to you what your seed is and ask Him to direct you to the best soil to plant it in. Keep in mind, you should always consider your local church as good soil to plant in. However, there are times God will instruct you to also plant seed into other ministries or other people that have blessed you in some form or another. Just be willing to be directed by Him and be sure to obey Him by doing what He said. (Isaiah 1:19)

From this day forward I encourage you to never pray for things again. You should pray for seed and seed or sow for things. God sent Jesus as His best seed into this Earth. Once Jesus died, and rose again that gave us the ability to become born-again, which produced Christians, which means to be Christ-like. God desired more of

Himself, so he sowed into the Earth His only begotten son made just like Him in order to produce more sons (Romans 8:14). This is showing us that God doesn't meet needs He meets seed, and seed produces harvest. He is the Lord of your Harvest.

Now, let's talk about the soil that's within you. Matthew 13:23(NLT) says:

The seed that fell on good soil represents those who truly hear and understand God's word and produce a harvest of thirty, sixty, or even a hundred times as much as had been planted.

Remember your words are seeds, and the best words you can speak is the Word of God. You have a garden, the Garden of Eden within your spirit or heart. All you have to do is put Word seed on the inside of you, and refuse to plant anything else so a harvest can be produced on the outside in your life. Your economy, the economy of God is on the inside of you. Please know your natural city is not your economy. Your economy begins and starts in the spirit realm. You are a God kind of creature with God kind of features. You and I were not born to settle for less and to live in mediocrity. We were not born to stay in lack, but we were born to live in surplus and abundance. We were born to be above only and not beneath, and to win and succeed in every area of our lives. Glory to God!

If you're broke financially it may be because your economy on the inside is not being richly supplied with the Word of God, with finance seed. Broke thinking produces a broke lifestyle. Proverbs 23:7a says:

For as he thinketh in his heart, so is he.

You may be asking, Tariq how can you think in your heart? I'm glad you asked. You are a tri-part being. You are a spirit, you have a soul, and you live in a physical body. (1 Thessalonians 5:23) Your soul is made up of your mind, will, and emotions; or your thinker, your chooser, and your feeler. Your soul is in your spirit so you think on the inside of the real you. What's in your head is your brain and your soul sends signals to your brain, which then tells your body what to do or how to feel. My goodness are you getting this? This is why we must renew our soul. So it can line up with our reborn spirit and we can present our bodies as living sacrifices and that it can prove what is the acceptable and perfect will of God for our lives (Romans 12:2).

So if you're rich on the inside, guess what? You're going to be rich on the outside. In your marriage or singleness. You're going to be rich at the credit union, You're going to be rich at the bank, and be rich with favor wherever you go. Friends, if you allow the Word to grow in your spirit which is your soil, whatever you touch will prosper.

As a man thinketh rich, as a man thinketh on the Word of God so shall he be. Your richness is on the inside of you. You are already complete. You are already wealthy, you have already been made complete. Maybe it doesn't seem like it to you, if not that's why you have to continually renew your mind in and through the Word of God. You must continue to discover who you really are, and how you were meant to function.

The Word of God has to become you. And once the Word becomes you, It will change your outside. The Word has the ability to change your life in one day. One can be broke one day and the next day be living in abundance. God has finished His part, it's on *your* willing and obedience now.

Reader, you are powerful! Continuously stay in the Word so you can continue to understand how powerful you really are. Remember, God doesn't meet needs, seed meets need. And harvest doesn't follow a need, harvest follows a seed. It's good to know that our Father *is* the Lord of the harvest.

The God-given Instructions You Obey Will Create Your Future!

The instructions that you obey from God will create *your* future. You must understand that the instructions you receive from God are tailor made for your life. Often times we're waiting for God to do something and we haven't invited Him in by asking for instructions or direction, especially in the area of finances. God knows which seed that you sow that will produce the harvest you need. With that being said, always ask God what to sow and where to sow. Paying your tithes is not considered sowing or an offering. The tithe belongs to God, it's what He requires from you. Your offering that you sow is above and beyond your tithe. Sometimes your seed may go higher than your tithe. For example, you made $800 this week and you put $80 on the envelope for tithe. That figure is already said and done. The word tithe literally means a tenth. Now, when you give an offering, you need to go to God and ask what amount to give in offering because His Word says, "will a man rob God in tithes and offerings" (Malachi 3:8-12). Once He ministers to you an amount, simply obey. It could be $160, $500, $50, $1,000 or it could be $5. Just don't throw money into the offering bucket. That's why many people haven't been receiving consistently, they've taken their offerings lightly and continue to keep just throwing money in any amount, anywhere. No, you have to get instructions, because if He tells you what to give then you better believe He has something for you. So ask God which seed will bring the desired harvest. There is a difference between throwing money in a bucket and obeying God. God watches over His word to perform it, not yours. (Jeremiah 1:12). Not your offering that you made up or the one that sounds good to you. God watches over His word, which are His instructions. He watches over to see your obedience in what He instructed you to give and do. If you get God's word on the issue then you have God on the issue. If you get God's instructions on your financial issue, you've got your answer for your financial issue. Notice I said God's word and God's instruction.

The only harvest God is obligated to give you is the one in which He directs your seed. Not the one you think you should sow. But yes, the one that He tells you to sow!

We know that all things are accessed through seed and God gives you the seed. Let' read 2 Corinthians 9:10 (NLT). It says:

For God is the one who provides seed for the farmer and then bread to eat. In the same way, he will provide and increase your resources and then produce a great harvest of generosity in you.

This is good news! He doesn't make you come up with the seed you need to sow He supplies it. It's simply up to you to obey His instructions with the seed He provides. You see God is not only the Lord of the Harvest, He's the Lord of the seed. Seedtime and harvest is how we operate in the Kingdom of God. Genesis 8:22 says:

While the earth remaineth, seedtime and harvest, and cold and heat, and summer and winter, and day and night shall not cease.

The moment God gives you the seed, in His mind you've got the harvest. He loves us so much that He believes we will already obey His instruction before He's even ministered it to us. So you've already got your harvest. The moment you receive any seed to sow, in God's mind you have the harvest. The reason you don't get the harvest is because you don't take time to get the instructions from Him, or you don't obey the instructions you were given.

Many times God has given His people the seed for what they are believing for but as soon as they get the seed they don't do anything with it. Are you getting this? See God see's you with the harvest. God is saying, "I did everything for you. I'm going to give you more, I'm going to allow seed to come, but you have a part to play, and your part is your obedience". You have to believe that God can and will speak to individuals to give you seed to sow. Every time someone gives to you it's not always your harvest, sometimes it's the seed that you need to sow for your harvest. He may speak to someone to sow into you $1,000. First, and foremost, tithe your 10% to your local church. You should purpose in your heart to tithe off of all your increase, not just employment increase such as your weekly check. Your tithe is the part that has already been instructed by God in His Word. However, you must decide to go to God to get instructions on the $900 that's left. Remember, your sowing of seed goes way farther than just going out and spending money will.

Reader, I declare over you right now that more seed is going to come your way. And because you choose to obey God's instructions, harvest is coming your way too. God sees you with it. It doesn't matter what age you are, what job you work now, you already have it in the spirit and if you obey, it's a done deal in the natural. Distractions, chaos, and confusion are sent into your life by satan so you can stop confessing the harvest of what you have sown for. It's important not to take your eyes off of the Seed Supplier, Instruction Giver, and Harvest Releaser which is God! For example, Peter was on the water focused on the Lord. But we know, as soon as the wind became boisterous he took his eyes off of who? The Lord. And as soon as he took his eyes off of the Instruction Giver he began sinking (Matthew 14:29-30). Same as your finances. Bills, debt, and lack can only sink you if you get your focus off of The Lord of the Harvest, the one who loves you. Those negative things come to choke the expectation of your harvest. They come to get you to become joyless and to deposit fear in you that tries to convince that God can't and won't do what He said He would do. Fear contaminates your faith in the waiting period of your harvest. Fear is simply: False Evidence Appearing Real. Fear is designed to rob you from the desired harvest in your life. 2 Chronicles 26:5 (AMP) says:

He set himself to seek God in the days of Zachariah who instructed, him in the things of God and as long as he sought (inquired of, yearned for) the Lord, God made him prosper.

Sounds like Zachariah received instructions. Right? God instructed Zechariah and because he obeyed the instructions, God made Him prosperous. The instructions you receive from God that you obey too, will make you prosper in all you do. Lets go to Job 36:11, it says:

If they shall obey and serve Him they shall spend their days in prosperity and their years in pleasantness and joy.

Glory to God! This scripture tells us our obedience to God and us serving in the Kingdom of God releases prosperity and makes our lives pleasant and joyful. Now, let's look at Job 36:12, it says:

If they obey not they shall perish by the sword of God's destructive judgment and they shall die in ignorance of true knowledge.

I don't know about you, but I'm not perishing, I've decided to obey in order to spend all my days in prosperity. I know firsthand, it's not always convenient to sow but it's always beneficial to. Hosea 4:6a says:

My people perish for a lack of knowledge.

We must understand, the scripture doesn't say the people of God perish for a lack of money, it says we perish from a lack of knowledge. A lack of knowledge is also known as a lack of obedience in instruction. Isaiah 1:19 says:

If ye be willing and obedient, ye shall eat the good of the land.

According to this scripture you can have two people in the same service that may hear the same word yet one of them still may struggle. Only the one who is willing and obedient will eat the good of the land.

Many times the instructions don't make sense, but keep in mind they make results. And the majority of times when God tell you to do something you don't have the money to do it. I sign off on that one. Just know that he will provide the seed, He's Jehovah Jireh, the Lord who provides.

Let's look at an example of instructions that produce overflow. Luke 5:4-6 says:

Now when he had left speaking, he said unto Simon, Launch out into the deep, and let down your nets for a draught. And Simon answering said unto him, Master, we have toiled all the night, and have taken nothing: nevertheless at thy word I will let down the net. And when they had this done, they inclosed a great multitude of fishes: and their net brake.

Child of God, know that at the Lord's direction, and at the Lord's instructions that you obey will make this your net breaking season. I believe that in your obedience so much favor will invade and break into your life, just obey your instructions. Simon Peter's instructions he received didn't make sense to him or the other fishermen, but thank God Simon Peter decided to obey despite who didn't agree with the instructions, even himself. I've found that if you obey immediately it alleviates or stops the opportunity for you or others to talk you out of what God told or showed you to do. Luke 5:8 goes on to say:

And they beckoned unto their partners, which were in the other ship, that they should come and help them. And they came, and filled both the ships, so that they began to sink.

This is powerful! I'm here to tell you are going to get broke off from God to the point where you are going to have to tell your friends that they must come and help you, because you need help receiving goodness! Can you believe that good news? Glory to God!

Another example of instructions that led to a harvest to meet a need is found in Matthew 17:24-27. This is when Peter was with Jesus in Capernaum and they both had taxes due. Jesus gave Peter specific instructions to meet the need. Jesus told Peter to go fish, and to take up the first fish that he caught, and when he would open up the fish mouth he would find a piece of money that would pay both of their taxes. What an awesome way God met the need! Instructions were given to Peter and faith was involved which requires action (James 2:17). Are you getting this? Please know that Jesus was not poor when he walked the Earth. He was financially loaded and could have easily paid both Him and Peter's taxes, but instead He required Peter's obedience to His instructions. Same with you, God requires your obedience to His instructions. Deuteronomy 28:1 says:

If you fully obey the LORD your God and carefully keep all his commands that I am giving you today, the LORD your God will set you high above all the nations of the world.

Reader, when you decide to fully obey the Lord in His instructions, written and spoken, you will set yourself up for a life of total prosperity in the Earth. Remember, **The God-given Instructions *You* Obey, Will Create *Your* Future.**

The 1st step to Total Prosperity:
<u>Receive Jesus Into Your Life</u>

Simply pray this prayer:

Dear Heavenly Father,

I come to you in the name of Jesus. Your Word says...him that cometh to me I will in no wise cast out" (John 6:37), so I know You won't cast me out, but You take me in and I thank You for it. You said in Your Word, "Whosoever shall call upon the name of the Lord shall be saved" (Romans 10:13). I am calling on Your name, so I know You saved me now. You also said, "If thou confess with thy mouth the Lord Jesus, and shalt believe in thine heart that God hath raised him from the dead, thou shalt be saved. For with the heart man believeth unto righteousness; and with the mouth confession is made unto salvation" (Romans 10:9-10). I believe in my heart Jesus Christ is the Son of God. I believe that He was raised from the dead for my justification, and I confess Him now as my Lord. Your word says..."with the heart man believeth unto righteousness...and I do believe with my heart, I have now become the righteousness of God in Christ (2 Corinthians. 5:21). I declare I am now saved.

<u>Welcome to the family!</u>

Now that you're saved, I encourage you to get connected and dedicated to a Bible-based ministry that teaches the uncompromised Word of God with simplicity and understanding, a place where you can grow into the things of God. Congratulations! You've been reborn!

-Pastor Tariq Price

... ...

www.ingramcontent.com/pod-product-compliance
Lightning Source LLC
La Vergne TN
LVHW051815080426
835513LV00017B/1972